Exploring the Arts

LISTENING TO MUSIC

by Chris de Souza

Marshall Cavendish · London · New York · Sydney · Toronto

Editorial Staff

Series Editor	Sue Lyon
Assistant Editor	Laura Buller
Art Editor	Helen James
Production Manager	Isabel Cossar
Managing Editor	Alan Ross
Editorial Consultant	Maggi McCormick

Library Edition published 1989
Published by Marshall Cavendish Corporation
147 West Merrick Road
Freeport, Long Island
N.Y. 11520

Typeset by J&L Composition Ltd,
Filey, North Yorkshire
Printed in the USA by Worzalla Publishing
Company, Wisconsin

Library of Congress Cataloging-in-Publication Data

Sousa, Chris de.
    Listening to music/Chris de Sousa.
          p.   cm. — (Exploring the arts)
    Bibliography: p.
    Includes index.
    ISBN 1–85435–104–4. — ISBN 1–85435–101–X (set): $85.00
    1. Music appreciation—Juvenile literature. I. Title.
II. Series.
MT6.S686   1989   89–7119
781.1′7—dc20   CIP
                                          AC MN

    ISBN 1–85435–101–X (set)
    ISBN 1–85435–104–4 (vol)

Contents

Introduction

Music is an international language. People all over the world organize the sounds around them into musical patterns to express their ideas and feelings. You can play music, sing music, or simply listen. Best of all, you can learn how to enjoy music.

This book will introduce you to the excitement of music. You will discover how music developed through time. You will also see how professional composers write music, and learn about the instruments that make up a modern orchestra. You will also find out about the different forms of music.

You can be a part of making music, too. Discover how to create music yourself with your own instruments, and how to compose your own simple music. With music, you can express yourself or enjoy yourself — just listen!

Stop and Listen

The world is full of noises. Just open your window and listen to them all! Try to separate all the noises from each other. Everything has its own noise, which you can hear if you listen hard enough. Just as you can recognize a thing by its color and shape, you can also recognize it by its sound.

Noises are all different, and you can distinguish them in three ways. They are either higher or lower in pitch (think of the difference between a man and a woman talking); or they are longer or shorter in duration (for example, the difference between a car passing and a tap on the door); or they are louder or softer in dynamics (for example, a train passing nearby or one passing far away). Every noise you hear is a mixture of these three things: pitch, duration, and dynamics.

Listen to all the sounds around you. Make a list of them, dividing them into louder, longer, and lower sounds or softer, shorter, and higher ones.

How you hear sound

When you make a noise – for example, when you clap your hands – the air around your hands moves away in invisible waves. Although you cannot see this, the air around you is full of invisible movement, similar to that made by waves in water. Some of these air waves are sound waves. When the waves reach your ears, your ears turn them into electrical impulses which travel into your brain. Your brain acts like a computer, and interprets them, telling you what sort of sound you are hearing. If

it is too loud, your brain will tell you to cover your ears with your hands to protect them. If the noise is very soft, your brain will tell you to cup your hand around your ear to help you focus the sound better. If the noise is made by something dangerous, such as a car speeding straight at you, your brain will tell you to run out of the way.

Do you want to hear all those sounds coming in through your window? Are they agreeable or disagreeable? If you do not want to listen to them, you can close your window and most of the sound waves will stay outside. But they will still make the window vibrate a little. The vibration will make the air in the room move around you, and you will still be able to hear the sounds outside, although they will now be muffled. The window is like a breakwater in the ocean: on one side, the water is rough; and on the other, it is smoother and calmer. On one side of your window, the air waves are strong; on the other, they are weaker, unless you make a lot of noise in your room!

Organized sound

Well, with all that noise going on, why do we want music? After all, it is only more noise. But music is very different from the noise outside your window. The noise outside is confused and disorganized and can often be very annoying. Musical noise is organized and can be very pleasant. The difference between disorganized and organized sound is similar to the difference between a simple meal, such as

Low, long, soft

Low, long, loud   **High, long, loud**

4

a hamburger, and a meal which takes hours to prepare. Sounds have to be organized in order to become music, and they can have a very strong influence on you. They can make you tap your feet, or dance, or march; or they can make you feel sad or sleepy. This book explains how people use music in these different ways. People who organize sounds are called composers. It is easier to compose music than you might think, but some people have composed music in such a special way that their music is listened to all over the world, sometimes hundreds of years after they wrote it.

Composers imagine patterns of noises, or tunes, in their heads. Then, when they are sure how the patterns are made up, they write down a set of signs that tells musicians what instruments to play and how to make the special noise patterns the composers imagined. When we hear the sounds, we listen for the patterns the composers have invented, and these patterns affect us in different ways. If the composers use colorful, energetic sounds, they can excite us; or if they use complicated sounds, or sounds made purposely out of order, they can make us feel sad or thoughtful. In this book, we will see how composers from the past and present have made musical patterns for us to listen to.

Some of the noises in this picture are described below. List others, saying whether they are high or low, long or short, loud or soft. Remember that quiet noises nearby sound louder than loud, distant ones.

High, short, loud   **Low, long, soft**   **High, long, very soft**   5

Sound Becomes Music

On the previous page, you found out that the world is full of noise and that music is organized sound. How did people decide what things to use to make their music?

Have you ever been doing something, such as woodworking or gardening, and suddenly found your hammer or shovel making a particular noise which catches your attention? Well, that is how the first people probably started to make music thousands of years ago.

Prehistoric people first made tools out of stone, wood, or bones, and, much later, with metal. Perhaps, when they were using their stone hammers, wooden spears, or bone cups, they discovered the different noises

they could make. It was not long before they used the noises their work tools made to make music as they worked, and they probably sang, too. The beat or rhythm of the music would have made the work easier. As the centuries went by, they began to adapt their tools in different ways so that they would make especially pleasant noises. They discovered that different-sized clay or wooden pots made different sounds when they were hit, and that if they covered them with animal skins, they made very good drums. Seed pods made good rattles. They discovered how to make hollow bones and reeds into pipes. In this

way, everyday objects that had started off as weapons or tools became musical instruments.

From bow to harp
When people started to hunt with bows and arrows, perhaps they discovered that the string of the bow made a twangy sound. If the bow was tight, the twangy sound was high in pitch; a loose bow made a lower twang. Soon, they began to make a different type of bow just to play as a twangy instrument. The next step was to give it more strings so it could make a range of notes. However, the sound still did not have much power. Then, people discovered that if they put a hollow piece of wood at the base of the bow, this would act as a soundbox and would make the noise louder. Soon, the strength of the strings on the musical bow became too

Above: The history of the harp.
a) A simple, one-stringed bow.
b) An ancient Egyptian harp with more strings and a soundbox.

c) An Egyptian harpist.
d) A medieval harp with a supporting strut on the third side.
e) A modern orchestral harp.

strong for the wood, and another piece of wood was added to stop the bow from collapsing. This began the development of the modern harp.

Some early harps were discovered recently in an Egyptian pyramid, where they had been buried with a king about 5,000 years ago.

On pages 22 and 23, you can see what some present-day string instruments look like. Of course, their soundboxes are much more complicated than the early ones.

Steel bands
Nowadays, people are very sure about what they consider to be a musical instrument. In fact, however, anything can be used as an instrument to make interesting sound or music.

A recent example of the way a modern "tool" has turned into a very exciting musical instrument is the use of the oil drum in the West Indian steel band. The workers in the oilfields in Trinidad turned empty oil drums upside down, and used them as musical drums. Soon, they found that they could make these oil drums play different notes by dividing the top of the drum into a pattern of different-sized shapes; each part of the pattern would make a different note when hit. By using many drums, they could play whole tunes.

Make your own steel band
There are probably many tools in your house that would make interesting instruments. Some composers have used anvils, saws, and garden hoses! Make your own steel band out of some empty coffee cans. Make sure you ask an adult to help you first. Draw simple patterns on the bottom of each can. For example, you could divide the base into three different-sized segments. Put them over a post or block of wood one by one and, with a hammer and blunt steel tool, tap along the lines you have drawn. When you hit different parts of the pattern with a hard stick, they will make musical noises.

Above: A West Indian steel band. Can you see the different shapes that have been beaten out on the oil drums? The smaller shapes on the shorter drum (right) make higher notes. Some of the big drums (back) give only one or two low notes, and two or three are used by one man. The drum on the right is divided into several segments, so the player can play a tune on his single drum.

The Power of Music

You have read how people used their instruments to make music while they worked and how the music helped them work. This is a good example of the power music can have. Primitive people in tribal societies today still use music to help them in their daily life. They have songs for walking, songs for playing – and music for making babies sleep! Perhaps the most common of all are working songs, such as those sung by laborers in Nigeria.

Can you imagine a world without music? The power of music is something most people need, though they may not always be aware of it. We have music wherever we go: in stores, restaurants, churches, schools, waiting rooms, sports events, in cars, and wherever we can take our radios and personal cassette players. Lively music may be used to make people work faster in factories; slow music can lull you into buying more food in a supermarket. We can use the power of music to entertain or relax us, or to help us express our feelings.

Making magic
In many parts of Africa and the Orient, people believe that music has magical powers, capable of healing illnesses and calling up evil or good spirits. Music is still used in this way in some tribes. A good example of the use of the power of music in a religious ceremony today is that of the Whirling Dervishes in Turkey. They whirl around and around for hours on end until they forget who or where they are, and they are in a complete frenzy. People do almost the same thing when

Above: The Whirling Dervishes perform their ritual dance.

they go to a rock concert. Loud music with a strong, repeated beat acts on us like a drug: it sets our hearts and pulses beating faster and faster. It gets us to move in time, tapping our feet, or jumping up and down, and it helps us to forget our worries.

If this happens to a whole group of people at the same time, it has an even more magical effect. Everyone may feel happy to be together, or the music may make a whole crowd of people act

Right: The Pipes and Drums of the Second Battalion of the Scots Guards march from the Wellington Barracks in London.

Above: John Philip Sousa (1854–1932)

Left: Modern ballroom dancers get a great thrill out of performing on the dance floor.

National music

People in different countries have their own style of music to excite them. Dance music shows the different national styles very clearly. Many composers have used the tunes and rhythms of their country in their own music to show how much they loved their own land. Some composers have even started a national style of music. The American John Philip Sousa was one of these. He is most famous for his marches. Sousa gave new vitality to the simple military march, and by the turn of the 20th century, his popularity as a composer and bandleader had spread worldwide. His marches included *Semper Fidelis*, *The Washington Post*, and the *Liberty Bell*, but his *Stars and Stripes Forever* was so well-loved that it is now almost like a national anthem to Americans.

like stampeding cattle. People get a thrill out of singing together around the campfire, for instance. They also get excited by watching marching bands step by in parades, and feel very proud as their national anthem is being played. Military marches help people go bravely to the dangers of war, and funeral marches help them get over the shock of losing friends and relatives. Music helps religious services to be solemn or joyful. It also helps people feel relaxed at parties.

Experimenting with Sound

Look around any room in your home. You can probably find a great many objects which can make very interesting noises. Almost anything in a house can be used to provide a noise! If you put a few objects together, you can make your own very special type of band. You can arrange the noisemakers into different groups, depending on what they are made of (for example, wood, metal, pottery, or glass) or how you make a noise with them (for example, blowing, scraping, or shaking). You can bang wood together, blow across the top of glass bottles, rattle a can with buttons inside, or scrape pieces of metal together. If the object is made of glass or metal, the sound it makes when you hit it will probably be a longish noise, similar to a bell or gong being struck.

If you hang a metal object on a loose piece of string, the noise it makes when you strike it will last longer because there is nothing to stop the metal from vibrating when you hit it. The vibrations make the air around the object move until the sound reaches your ear. If the vibrations are stopped, the noise will stop. Look carefully at the metal after you have hit it and you will see it shaking very fast; if you touch it with something soft, it will stop

sounding because the vibrations have been stopped. The noise anything makes also depends on what you hit it with.

Experiment with all kinds of different materials to see which ones make the most interesting sounds. Then make a list of the ones you like best, and why. It is great fun to make music this way. It will not sound like "normal" music, but it certainly is music because you have organized it especially for fun.

Organize your sounds

Now, you can organize your collection of sound makers. Decide which ones to sound, how you want them to sound, what other sounds to play with them,

Right: To play this musical game, you will need some playing cards and dice. Each color on the board stands for a noise. Give each noisemaker (examples are given below) a separate color – for example, green for bottles, red for cups. When you land, pick up a card, and make the noise the same number of times as the number on the card.

4	3 Miss a turn	2
5 Move four squares forward	6	7
14	13	12
15	16 Go back to start	17
24	23	22

Left: A page of the performance score for Stockhausen's *Kontakte* for electronic sounds, piano, and percussion. The top part between the two thick lines is a "picture" of the electronic tape sounds. The middle band of notes is for the percussion player and the lowest band is for the pianist. On this page, the pianist starts off by playing percussion as well (bottom left), but then plays piano (bottom right).

how long the sounds should last (duration), or how loud or soft they should be (dynamics). How many players do you need? You can make different patterns of sound just like a professional composer does.

Writing down sound

Then, also as a composer does, you can write your patterns down on paper to remind you if you want to play them again. For each sound you make, invent a shape and a color in which to draw it. A bright, bell-like sound could have a clear shape on paper, a softer or a lower sound could look more like a smudge. What kind of shapes do you think your various noises make? What color is the sound of a can rattling? Once you have decided how to represent your sounds, you can make up patterns on paper. Then, by reading the patterns one by one, you can play your music. Patterns on paper to represent sounds are called scores. Many modern composers have invented their own way of writing down sounds.

Musical games

Another way of organizing sounds is to arrange musical games. Some composers like to have surprises in their music. They make up a set of rules or instructions to players which allows them a great deal of choice of what and how to play. Because this music also has an element of chance, no two performances are ever the same. There is a number of chance elements in Karlheinz Stockhausen's music, an example of which is at the top of the page. You can invent your own games of chance using cards or dice, like the one on the left.

Musical objects

Professional composers have used many of the noises of the everyday world in their music. Giuseppe Verdi used blacksmiths' anvils in *Il Trovatore*; Richard Wagner in *The Rhine Gold* did the same. Gustav Mahler used a hammer and cowbells in his *Sixth Symphony*, and George Gershwin used car horns in *An American in Paris*. Now that we can record any noise on tape, composers also use taped sounds in their music. Some even use computers to control electronic instruments and to help them compose.

Keeping in Time

When you were making up your music with your group of sound makers, you probably noticed that one of the most important things to do was to decide how long each noise should last. Some sounds are much longer than others. But how can you show which is which on paper in your score?

Dividing time

If you divide your score up into equal spaces and call each space a second, or any other measure of time you like, then you can draw each sound pattern to cover as many spaces as you want it to last. Four spaces means the sound could last for the count of four, or four seconds. Instead of having to watch a clock to count your beats, you could have someone else beating time while you play. Musicians often use a metronome, a machine which can be set to make anything from one to over 200 beats a minute.

Inventing different patterns of rhythm can be fun, too. Try clapping your hands twice to each of your foot stamps. Or you could divide each beat by clapping your hands three, four, or five times to each foot stamp. If you listen carefully, most music divides itself up into groups of two, three, or four beats. Marching or walking music has to be in two or four time. More complicated movements such as dance steps are often in groups of three.

Different note shapes, such as whole notes and half notes, were invented in the 12th century to show the lengths of the notes compared with each other. Each note is worth two of the next. To write down notes worth three of the next, shorter note, you simply

Above: François Couperin (1668–1733)

add a dot. A dotted whole note is worth three half notes, a dotted half note three quarter notes, and so on. As many dances have beats grouped into three, this "musical

Above: Maelzel's metronome. The "wedge" on the lever is a weight. The higher you put the weight, the slower it ticks.

Right: A quarter note without a dot is worth two eighth notes. Adding a dot makes it worth three.

Dance patterns

Most of the instrumental music you hear is based on old dance patterns. The most important ones were developed in France in the 17th and 18th centuries. Two of the greatest composers of that time were François Couperin and Jean Philippe Rameau. Like many composers of that time, they composed groups of different types of dances called suites. People at court did not dance to these suites, but sat and listened to them as concert music.

One of the most important dances of the time was the minuet. When the French settled in America and built the city of New Orleans in the late 17th century, they took the minuet with them. There, the old, stately minuet gradually became faster until it became the modern jive associated with rock and roll.

shorthand" is useful.

You can make a musical "ruler" similar to the one above, to show how the notes relate to each other. Just as there are 12 inches to a foot, so there are a certain number of eighth notes to a quarter note, so patterns may be repeated.

Top: A stylized jive sequence from the musical *West Side Story*. Steady rhythms of older dances gave way to more energetic steps.

Above: A musical "ruler." The whole note at the top is two half notes, four quarter notes, eight eighth notes, or 16 sixteenth notes.

Musical Codes

When you learn a tune to sing, one way of learning it is to listen to someone else play it and then try to remember it. If it is a long tune, this can be quite difficult, and some music is so complicated you could not learn it in this way.

For hundreds of years, until monks invented ways of writing music in the eighth century, singers in church or court singers had to learn music by heart. As tunes became more complicated, monks started to use signs called neumes to show whether the tune or melody went up or down, to help the memory. Soon, even this was not enough. About 300 years later, musicians added a line going right across the page to show where a particular note, such as middle C, was. Once this line was drawn, they started to add more and more lines until all the notes had a line, or a space in between the lines. Musicians no longer guessed their notes, they had a very exact musical alphabet.

Musical alphabet
At the top of the diagram, you can see that the musical alphabet only goes up to G, then starts all over again. That is because every eighth note sounds like the first note, but eight notes higher or lower; so for that reason, it can have the same name. Most music was sung at first, so the lines and spaces (or staves) they used covered roughly all the notes from the lowest note a man could sing to the highest a woman could. To make it clearer which was which, musicians put clefs at the beginning of the staff to show at what pitch the notes should be sung. The bass clef, developed from an old way of writing F,

shows where the F line is. The treble clef shows where the G line is. Musicians sometimes used a C clef (which shows where middle C is), halfway between the bass and treble clef, for middle voices such as tenors or altos.

Since each note was named after a letter of the alphabet, by the 16th century, musicians started to use the notes to spell words, using the first seven letters of the alphabet. The words could give them an interesting tune. You can do it, too. Words such as *bed* or *cage* are easy. If you have a piano or recorder, play them and see how they sound. Some people can spell their names – can you?

Musical signatures
The German composer, Johann Sebastian Bach, could spell his name and, because he was famous, other composers have

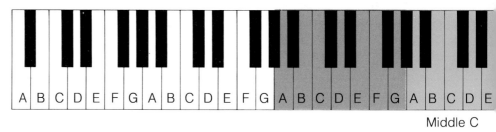

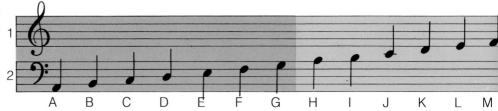

Above: At the top, piano keys are marked with their note names. Below the keyboard, the notes are shown on the treble (1) and bass (2) staves. Then, on the lower pair of staves, each note is given one of the letters of the whole alphabet.

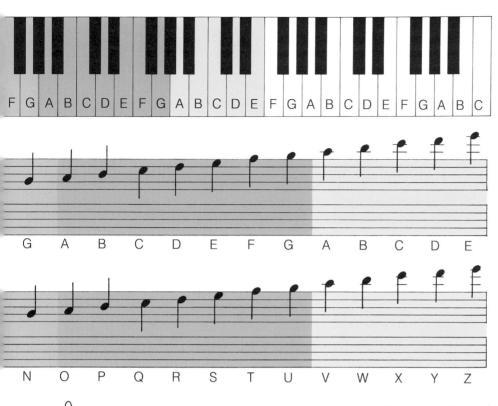

Above: Robert Schumann (1810–1856)

used his name as the start of a piece of music in his honor.

Even though he had an H in his name, Bach could spell it because the German musical alphabet uses another letter, H, for the note we call B. (The note they call B is the one we call B flat — halfway between A and B.)

Not all composers were as lucky as Bach. Another German composer, Robert Schumann, had a more difficult name to spell. However, he was lucky because the Germans also call the note E flat *Es*, so he used it as S because both have the same sound when pronounced. His musical letters, therefore, were *SCH*um*A*nn. Schumann liked playing musical word games. One of his girlfriends lived in a town called Asch. He used the town's name in a piece of music called *Carnaval* as a message to her.

Another composer who used musical codes was the Russian Dimitri Shostakovich. He used *S* in the same way as Schumann and got *D SCH*. These letters gave him a very individual tune which he used in much of his music as a kind of signature, similar to an artist's name on a painting.

The cleverest way to spell words in music is to give each note one of the letters of the whole alphabet. This means that an A can be H, O, or V; or a B an I, P, or W, and so on. The French composer Maurice Ravel used this method to pay tribute to another composer, Joseph Haydn. He remembered the German way of calling *B* an *H*, which solved the problem of spelling Haydn's name, in his *Minuet on the Name of Haydn*. This music was a double tribute because Haydn was a great composer of minuets, too. You can see how all these names appear in music on the left.

Left: The marks painted above the words on this 14th-century manuscript are neumes, an old form of writing music.
Below: Can you decode the musical sentence at the bottom of the page? The answer is on page 46.

Your Voice and Music

You have read how prehistoric people probably began to use tools as instruments; but, of course, their first instruments must have been their voices. The first music any person makes is by using the voice and other parts of the body, such as hands and feet. Listen carefully to anyone

speaking: you will hear the voice going up and down in pitch, using higher and lower notes. Some people use as many as five notes (called a fifth). Listen carefully as you speak, and see how many different notes you use.

Singing simply makes more of the notes than speaking, but sometimes the words stay on the same note, which is called chanting. Monks chant in church. This helps the sounds carry further, and also helps them concentrate on the meaning of the words they are chanting. Singing is much more controlled than speech. Unlike talking, singing has a very regular rhythm. Other people may often join in and enjoy being part of the group. This can happen when

people sing at family celebrations, on a long car journey, or around a campfire.

Folk songs
Folk songs were made up by ordinary people and passed down from generation to generation, to be sung on every kind of occasion. Now, we have radio and television, and people do not sing together as much as they used to. Just as all languages sound different from each other; so does the folk music of each country. This is because the song tunes have to follow the rise and fall (or lilt) and rhythm of speech.

Folk songs are very old tunes which have grown up with the words and have been handed down by memory. Around the

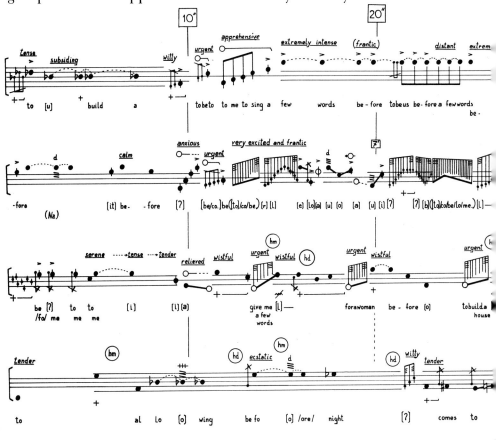

Left: Benedictine monks chanting. Monks such as these led the development of music from the 8th to the 15th centuries.

Above: A page from the score of Berio's *Sequenza III*. Every noise a person can make with their throat and mouth is used.

16

beginning of the 12th century in Europe in the rich palaces of kings and princes, professional songwriters started to compose brand new songs. To begin with, they were close to folk songs in style, but gradually, they became more and more complicated. These folk-style songs were often accepted as genuine folk songs by later generations. Examples are *Oh! Susanna* in America, *Rule Britannia* in Britain, *Silent Night* and *The Linden Tree* in German-speaking countries. *The Linden Tree* was written by Franz Schubert, who was probably the greatest songwriter of all time. He died when he was only 31, but in his short lifetime, he wrote over 900 songs. Some, such as *The Linden Tree*, are very simple, like folk songs, while others are very complicated, dramatic pieces.

Playing together

When you have a chance to listen to a singer accompanied by, for example, a piano, listen carefully to what the piano is playing underneath the voice part. This accompaniment often tells you more about the words. In Schubert's song *The Erl-King*, the piano suggests the galloping hooves of the horse as the father rushes home to try to save his son's life before the Erl-King (King of the Elves) catches him. Suddenly, the piano stops, and you know the boy is dead. The words tell the story, and the accompaniment sets the feeling or mood of the song.

Write your own song

Why not try to write a song? Make up a story about something frightening – about a storm, perhaps. Then invent some sounds with the sound makers you have collected to set a frightening or stormy mood to accompany your tune. Do not forget that your voice can also make noises such as growling, laughing, and tongue-clicking. Some modern composers use sounds like these in their music. Luciano Berio wrote a piece of music called *Sequenza III* which uses many varied sounds.

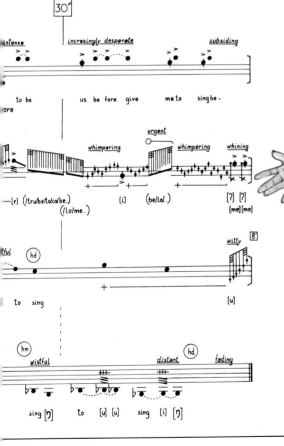

Right: A Bavarian folk singer and an accordion player in national costume. Every country has its own distinctive style of music.

17

The Percussion Family

On pages 6 and 7, you read how prehistoric people may have discovered music could be made by hitting one object against another. On pages 10 and 11, you probably found that this is the easiest way of making interesting sounds. The word percussion, meaning hitting, describes this kind of instrument. A percussion instrument can be made of metal, wood, stone, or animal skin and can be hit with any kind of object.

It is fairly certain that the first instruments were percussion ones. The first element of music is rhythm, and percussion instruments help make rhythm clearer. Very primitive music, such as music played by the Australian aborigines, is largely rhythmic. If you listen to the music of less primitive African tribes, you can see they have developed more complicated instruments that can play tunes as well as rhythms.

The percussion family

There are hundreds of different types of percussion instruments, but they can generally be divided into two groups; untuned ones that do not give a particular, set note, and tuned ones that do. Then, you can divide each of these groups into three further groups depending on whether they are metal (for example, bells or gongs), wood (for example, rattles), or any other natural material such as bone, stone, or skin (for example, drums). Which groups do your sound makers belong to?

Over the centuries, basic, untuned rhythm-making percussion instruments have developed into modern, tuned,

melody-making ones, such as the xylophone. These developments show how music has moved from primitive rhythms to highly-organized sound patterns where rhythm and melody have equal importance.

The story of the drum

The first drums were probably made of hollow wood. Later, skins were stretched over hollow wooden or pottery bowls. This kind of drum would be more resonant (meaning the sound lasts longer and is more powerful) because skin vibrates more freely than wood. Players also found that the bigger the area of skin and the greater the depth of the bowl, the more booming the sound would be. The skin was kept tightly stretched by thongs tied around the underside of the drum. They also found out that the tighter the thongs were, the higher the note would be. If they made different drums to play different pitches, this helped make the rhythm patterns more interesting. By pressing the thongs or the skin while they played the drums, they could make the notes slide up or down a little. This kind of sound is very like the sound of the human voice speaking. Many African tribes used drums to send messages.

By the 17th century in Europe,

a pair of tuned drums were regularly played with trumpets and horns in military music. When brass instruments were

Cymbals

Pedal-tuned kettledrum

Above right: The layout of a modern orchestra. The colored area shows where the percussion players are placed.

Right: These instruments are used most often, but others, such as xylophones and gongs, can be added.

played indoors to accompany important state occasions, the kettledrums or timpani came with them. By the 1800s, two or three timpani were normally used in an orchestra. Timpani players (or timpanists) could make the loud passages of music very striking by playing single, loud notes. They could also add great weight to the sound by doing a drum roll, beating the two sticks so fast that they sounded like one, long note. When composers wanted more tuned drum notes, they added more drums, until the French composer, Hector Berlioz, used 16 timpani in his *Requiem* in 1837.

The note in this kind of drum is changed by turning screws around the edge of the drum to tighten the skin or head. There are also timpani with pedals, which make it easier to change the note very quickly, or even slide the note by changing it while doing a drum-roll. One of the first composers to use this sliding effect was the Hungarian Béla Bartók in his *Music for Strings, Percussion, and Celesta* in 1936.

In the last 100 years, quite a few composers have used percussion instruments such as xylophones, glockenspiels, and other tuned percussion. They have used hammers, anvils, percussion instruments from the Orient, and even glass bottles, teaspoons, and other pieces of silverware. Musicians who play in an orchestra call the percussion section the kitchen!

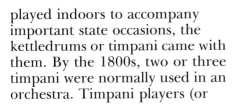

Bass drum

Hand-tuned kettledrum

Side drum

Triangle

Above: A homemade percussion band. You can make instruments like these and write music for your own group.

19

Keyboard Music

The piano is so well-known and widely used you might think it has been around for a long time. In fact, it is one of the most recently-invented instruments. The first keyboard instruments were primitive organs, which had very simple slides or levers to release the notes. The first keyboards on stringed instruments appeared in the 14th century. They were little, table-top spinets or virginals and had few notes. When you press a key on one of these instruments, a small plectrum plucks a string inside. This explains why a virginal sounds rather like a guitar, which is plucked, too. The early keyboard instruments were also much quieter than a modern piano.

In addition to the virginal, there was another bigger instrument called a harpsichord, which looks similar to a grand piano. The harpsichord was in popular use until the late 1700s. Composers such as Bach, Handel, Scarlatti, Rameau, and Couperin wrote their greatest works for it.

There was another, smaller instrument in use called a clavichord. It was very quiet, too, but sensitive to touch. Bach was very fond of it. When the key is pressed, it does not pluck the string as the harpsichord does. Instead, there is a little blade called a tangent to touch the string. As long as you press the key, the tangent stays against the string. This means you can make the note waver expressively and play it louder or softer.

The story of the piano

The piano got its name because it could also play softly (*piano* means soft in Italian). The first pianos, called *forte-pianos* or loud-softs (*forte* is Italian for loud) were invented around 1700. Bach played one, but at that time still preferred the clavichord. At the turn of the 18th century, the piano became more important through the music of Joseph Haydn, Wolfgang Amadeus Mozart (both from Austria), and the German composer, Ludwig van Beethoven. The piano's strings are hit, but each one is hit by a soft, felt-covered hammer which drops back as soon as the string has been hit. The sound continues as long as you hold the key down because another felt-covered stick called a damper stays away from the string until you let go, so the vibration continues. Then, when it touches the string, the sound is stopped or damped. Modern pianos are very powerful, with up to three strings for each note. As they became more powerful, composers wrote more and more difficult music for pianists and sometimes tried to make the piano copy the sound of a whole orchestra. The piano's full name became *pianoforte* at the beginning of the 19th century.

Frédéric Chopin and Franz Liszt are two particularly famous composers of piano music of the 19th century. Between them, they

Concert grand piano

Above: How a clavichord works. When you press the key (a) the tangent (b) strikes up against the string (c).

Above: When you press a key (a) on a harpsichord, a rod (b) lifts a plectrum (c), which plucks the string (d).

Above: When you press a piano key (a), a hammer (b) hits the string (c). A damper (d) lifts off the string to let it vibrate.

Harpsichord

Above: Frédéric Chopin (1810–1849)

developed a way of playing the piano that cannot really be bettered. Chopin wrote hardly any music for other instruments. He created a piano style, a way of using the keyboard, and a type of melody that people copied for the next 60 years. Although he lived nearly all his life away from his native Poland, Chopin always felt close to his country and wrote many pieces based on Polish dances, such as the *mazurka* and *polonaise*. His waltzes are also very popular.

Franz Liszt could not be more different from his friend Chopin. It is difficult to believe how much he crammed into his life. He traveled more, wrote more, helped other composers, and was a far better performer and more original composer than most other musicians. His music is still regarded as the most difficult to play. Much of it, called program music, describes a person, place, picture, or story. Liszt made the Hungarian style of music famous in his *Hungarian Rhapsodies*.

The String Family

On pages 6 and 7, you saw how the idea for a harp probably developed from the early hunting bow. Other stringed instruments may have developed from a bow, but, all have long, straight necks (which is usually where you finger the notes), a body which acts as a soundbox to make the vibrations travel further, and, of course, one or more strings stretched across the whole instrument over a bridge and tightened by pegs.

You can test this way of making music yourself. Stretch a rubber band between your fingers, pluck it, and listen to the noise it makes. The thicker the band, the lower the sound; the tighter the band, the higher. If you look carefully at a stringed instrument just after you have played it, you can see the strings vibrating very fast. The vibration makes the air around the string move in waves until it comes to your ear. The

shorter or tighter the cord, the faster it vibrates, and the faster or more frequently it vibrates, the higher the note.

Each musical note has its own special frequency. For example, the note A that you hear when an orchestra tunes up, has a frequency of 440 cycles or vibrations per second. If you make a string vibrate at twice that speed, or 880 cycles per second, it will be exactly one octave (eight notes) higher, and so on, up or down. The note an octave lower will vibrate at 220 cycles per second. Another way to raise the pitch of a note is to shorten the string by putting a finger or other kind of stop in the way.

The string family
The most common string instruments include the guitar and the violin. The guitar was first used many centuries ago. It

Double bass

Above: Make your own stringed instruments. Stretch rubber bands over a cereal box (cut out a semicircle for a bridge) or stretch a string from a pole set into a box to make a "double bass."

Above: Guitarist John Williams.

Above: The double bass is the biggest stringed instrument in the modern string family, and can play very low notes.

was brought to Spain in the ninth century from Arabia. Most guitars have six strings and a wide range of notes. Although the guitar is mainly thought of as Spanish, it has been a popular instrument all over Europe since the 18th century, when it became more popular than the lute and mandolin (there is a lute in the smaller illustration on page 34). Many composers wrote music for it, often in combination with flute or violin. The Italian Niccolò Paganini, who perhaps was the greatest violinist there has been, was also a very good guitar player and wrote many pieces for it. Like the lute or mandolin, it makes a very suitable accompaniment for a singer.

During the 15th and 16th centuries in particular, the most popular family of stringed instruments was the viol family. Although different in many ways, viols are similar in shape and size to the violin (you can see a bass viol being played on page 34), but are less powerful in sound. The viol fingerboard has ridges on it calld frets (guitars also have frets, like those on the guitar on the opposite page).

The violin, as we know it, first appeared in the 16th century, but has very old ancestors. Gradually the violin took over from the viol, especially in Italy. Composers such as Giuseppe Tartini and Arcangelo Corelli made the best use of the expressive violins being made by people such as the famous violin-maker Stradivari. By the middle of the 1700s, the full violin family of violin, viola, cello (violoncello in full), and double bass had almost completely taken over as the most popular group of stringed instruments.

Chamber music
In the princely courts of Europe, the entertainment was given by small groups of musicians in the salons or chambers, playing chamber music. The most important classical chamber music was the string quartet, with two violins, a viola, and a cello. Haydn was the great "father" of the quartet; he wrote more than eighty. He also wrote hundreds of other pieces of music for chamber groups formed with other kinds of instruments. Since then, the quartet has been thought of as the most important form of chamber music a composer can write.

Cello

Viola

Violin

Above: The violoncello (or cello for short). Its notes are not quite as low as a double bass, and it can play quite high ones.

Above: The viola (left) is only a little bigger than the violin, but has a mellower sound. It can play five notes lower.

Above: The orchestra layout showing where the string players sit (first and second violins, violas, cellos, and double basses).

23

The Wind Family

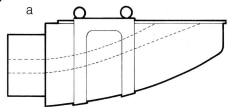

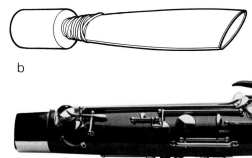

Pick up a glass bottle, or any bottle with a narrow neck-opening, and blow across the top; you will hear a quiet, humming sound. What you are doing is making the air inside vibrate against the side of the bottle. In turn, this makes the air outside vibrate and the sound waves travel to your ear. This is what happens in all wind instruments.

Good vibrations

The pitch of the note depends on the length of the column of air vibrating in the instrument, just as, on a stringed instrument, the pitch of the note depends on the length of the string. The first wind instruments were probably hollow bones, shells, gourds, or pottery imitations. Wood became the most usual material, so these instruments came to be described as woodwinds. Soon, people discovered that if holes were made in the tube and covered in various ways with fingers, the note would change. They found out how to hollow reeds and bamboos and tune them.

Another way to get the air to vibrate is by using a reed in the mouthpiece of the instrument. Put a blade of grass (or paper) between your two thumbs and blow through them. You should get a very piercing sound! This is how a reed works.

You can now divide woodwind instruments into two groups, open flue and reed. Recorders, flutes and even referees' whistles are flues; oboes, clarinets, and bagpipes are reed instruments. Reeds can be single, as in clarinets and saxophones, or double, as in oboes, their big cousin, the English horn, and the bassoon.

As we have already described, stopping the holes in a wind instrument changes the length of the vibrating air column. There is another way of doing this and that is by overblowing. If you blow harder than you need to, the instrument will play an octave higher at double the frequency, or vibrations per second. Some instruments have holes to help you do this.

Of course, some instruments are very big and have more holes than you have fingers. Over the years, a system of keys and levers has been developed to make it easy. The standard system today was invented by Theobald Boehm in about 1830, and makes very complicated and fast passages much easier. If you can already play a recorder, it would not take you long to learn the Boehm fingering on, for example, a clarinet or bassoon.

One of the oldest instruments is the panpipe; you can see these on vase paintings done over 2,500 years ago. Instead of having one tube with holes in it, the panpipe has many tubes of different lengths bound together, one tube for each note. Panpipes are still used in Rumanian folk music.

A musical genius

One of the very few composers (except for folk musicians) to use panpipes was Mozart, one of the most brilliant musicians who has ever lived. He began to play the harpsichord at the age of three and compose at five, and was a brilliant pianist and violinist. He

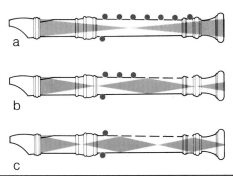

Above: With all holes covered (a), the air wave is as long as the tube. In (b) and (c), short, frequent waves make the notes higher.

Left: A single reed (a) and a double reed (b). There is a double reed on the bassoon. The position of the woodwinds in the orchestra is shown on the right.

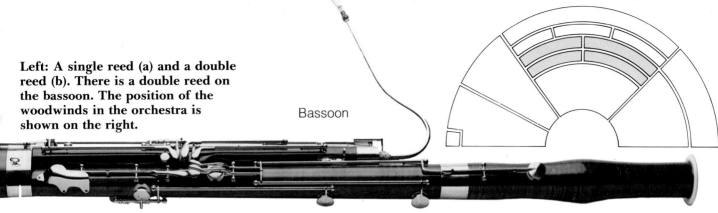

Bassoon

Clarinet

Oboe

Flute

knew Haydn and played quartets with him. In Mozart's opera *The Magic Flute*, Prince Tamino is on a difficult journey to rescue Princess Pamina. Three spirits give him a magic flute to protect him, and give his companion Papageno some magic bells. Papageno is a bird-catcher and has a panpipe to help him catch birds and to signal to Tamino.

Make your own panpipe by cutting up different lengths of hollow reed or bamboo and binding them together. Blow across the tops just as you blew across the glass bottle and they will make sounds.

Left: A group or consort of recorders. The usual combination is, from left to right: descant, treble, tenor, and bass recorders.

Above: A performance of Mozart's *The Magic Flute*. Papageno is playing his panpipe to catch birds. In the background

is the dead dragon that threatened the hero, Prince Tamino. Papageno pretends that he killed it, but turns out to be a coward.

The Brass Family

Brass instruments are wind instruments made of metal (not always brass); but the basic difference between brass and woodwind instruments is the mouthpiece. When you blow into a brass one, it makes your lips vibrate in the same way as the reeds of an oboe or bassoon.

Hidden notes

All brass instruments have a simple tube. Each tube produces a series of notes. This series varies according to the length of the tube. Every length of tube has a fundamental note which actually contains the sounds of the notes in its series. This is called the harmonic series.

The fundamental note (the first note in the series) is the first harmonic; the second harmonic (the second note) has twice as many vibrations and is an octave higher; the third harmonic (the third note) has three times as many vibrations and is an octave and five notes higher; the fourth has four times the vibrations and is two octaves higher, and so on. The higher up the series you go, the closer the notes are together until, at the top, you actually get a series of notes one note apart, called a scale. These high notes are difficult to blow and so early brass instruments had to make do with the few notes at the bottom of the series, which do not make a complete scale. That is why a simple instrument such as the bugle plays fanfares using so few notes. Some composers, such as Bach in his second Brandenburg concerto (see page 32), have used the difficult top notes to write brilliant trumpet tunes.

In order to make a brass instrument that could play all the notes of the scale from the lowest to the highest, it was necessary to change the length of the tube. Then the instrument could play the harmonic series of the seven fundamentals from A to G. To lengthen the tube, extra pieces called crooks were added to it. Of course, this took time, so that neither trumpets nor horns played very complicated tunes until the invention of valves.

Making it easier

Valves have made it possible to change the length of a tube at the press of a finger. Valves for brass instruments were invented around 1800. Connected to each valve is a separate length of tube, similar to the old crook, which is added to the main tube when the valve is pressed. By using three valves in various combinations, you can get all seven lengths.

Trombones have always been different. They have a slide which alters the length of the tube instantly. They can play any of the seven fundamental notes by

Tuba

Trumpet

Trombone

Diagram of trumpet

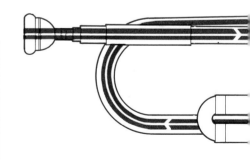

Middle C

Above: Magic sounds! Press the notes marked x, y, and z on a piano without making them sound, then play the one marked A and let it go. Notes x, y, and z will be heard quietly because they are part of the harmonic series of A. This also works in reverse. **Above: In this diagram, you can see how air travels through the tubes of a trumpet from the mouthpiece when different notes**

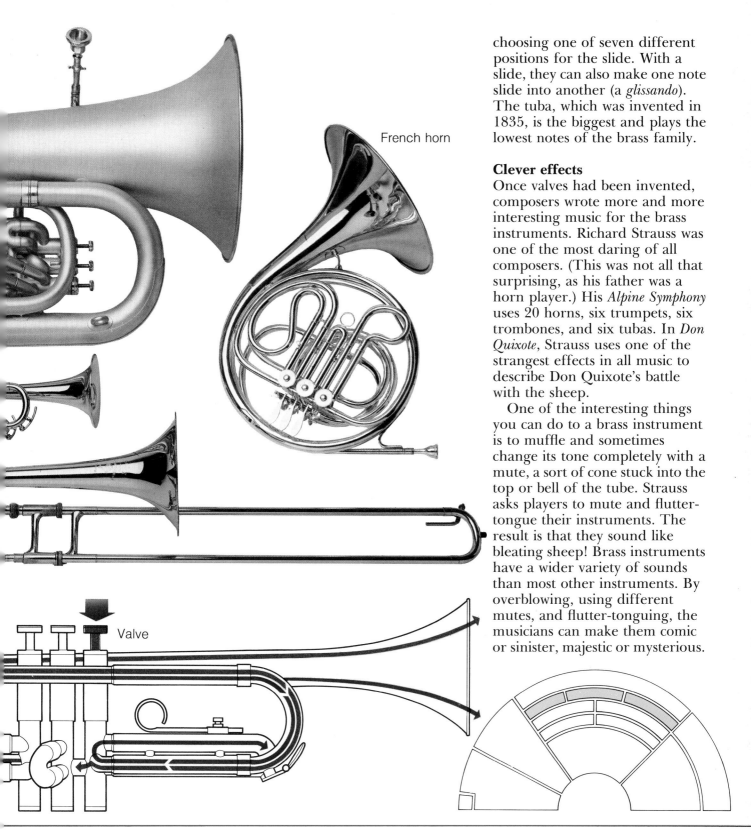

French horn

Valve

choosing one of seven different positions for the slide. With a slide, they can also make one note slide into another (a *glissando*). The tuba, which was invented in 1835, is the biggest and plays the lowest notes of the brass family.

Clever effects

Once valves had been invented, composers wrote more and more interesting music for the brass instruments. Richard Strauss was one of the most daring of all composers. (This was not all that surprising, as his father was a horn player.) His *Alpine Symphony* uses 20 horns, six trumpets, six trombones, and six tubas. In *Don Quixote*, Strauss uses one of the strangest effects in all music to describe Don Quixote's battle with the sheep.

One of the interesting things you can do to a brass instrument is to muffle and sometimes change its tone completely with a mute, a sort of cone stuck into the top or bell of the tube. Strauss asks players to mute and flutter-tongue their instruments. The result is that they sound like bleating sheep! Brass instruments have a wider variety of sounds than most other instruments. By overblowing, using different mutes, and flutter-tonguing, the musicians can make them comic or sinister, majestic or mysterious.

are played. The red arrows show how the air travels around when all the valves are up. The blue arrows show what happens when

the valve on the right is pressed down. The flow of air is diverted, and a lower note or series of notes can be made.

Above: The position of the brass instruments in the orchestra: horns on the left, trumpets next, trombones and tubas on the right.

The Orchestra

We usually know exactly what we mean when we talk about an orchestra today. It is a group of about 60 musicians playing all the most important instruments in the wind, brass, string, and percussion families. A hundred years ago, orchestras were much smaller; and 200 years ago, they were made up of whatever players were available, never more than 30. Haydn usually wrote his first orchestral music around 1750 for a small group of strings with one flute, two oboes, a bassoon, and two horns. By 1790, clarinets had come to stay. In the early 1800s, Beethoven added a third horn, in his third symphony, and then trombones in his fifth. More strings were now needed to balance these extra wind and brass instruments: between 16 and 20 violins, six to eight violas and cellos, with up to ten double basses.

By the late 19th century, when composers such as Richard Wagner and Richard Strauss started regularly using 25 or more brass and wind instruments, orchestras grew to over 100 players. Strauss's *Alpine Symphony* uses 130. It is very expensive to have such a large orchestra today, and composers have started writing for smaller groups. The orchestra is here to stay, though, because so much music for symphony orchestras was written between 1750 and the early 1900s. Most big towns and opera companies have their own orchestras. Many orchestras help pay for themselves by making records and film soundtracks as well as giving concerts.

The instruments
The strings are the main group of instruments. The string players sit in front of the louder instruments, divided into two groups. The first violins usually play the important tunes, but sometimes change with the second violins sitting behind or opposite them. The leader of the first violins is also called the concertmaster, and is almost as important as the conductor. The violas play the middle harmonies with the second violins, and the cellos play the bass notes. The double basses usually play the same notes as the cellos, but an octave lower.

The woodwinds sit in the middle of the orchestra with the flutes on the left side. The brass

Piano (Soft)　　Pizzicato (Plucked)　　Dolce (Sweetly)

Above center: The layout of a modern orchestra often looks like this. Percussion players often play more than one instrument.

☐ Harpist		☐ Violas
▨ Concertmaster		■ Cellos
☐ First violins		■ Double basses
☐ Second violins		☐ Flutes

28

sit behind the woodwinds and, the noisiest of all, the percussion are right at the back.

Molto doloroso
(Very sadly)

Con forza
(Forcefully)

The conductor

With so many musicians to keep together, orchestras usually have someone to beat time in front of them. Two hundred years ago, the conductor also played the violin or the harpsichord with the orchestra but, as music became more and more complicated, he had to concentrate on directing the other musicians. In addition to keeping time, starting and stopping the players together, and reminding them to go slower or faster as the composer requires, a conductor also interprets the music. He tells the players how he thinks the composer wanted it to sound (words such as those on the left are written over the music), and listens carefully to the balance of the instruments. The conductor even shows them the best way of playing a tricky passage and tries to inspire them with the mood of the piece. Conductors have to have exceptionally good hearing and usually have worked in orchestras before they start to direct them. Sometimes, though, conductors start conducting right from the start. The best conductors can usually learn by heart the music for all the instruments playing a particular piece of music.

Beating time

Beating time is quite simple; look at the diagrams and see how to beat two, three, or four beats to a

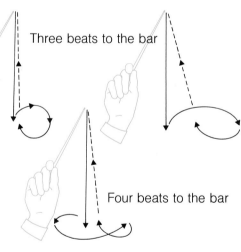

Two beats to the bar

Three beats to the bar

Four beats to the bar

bar. Depending on where the conductor's hand is, the players can tell what beat of the bar they should be on. If he makes large moves, this is a signal for the musicians to get louder; if he makes little ones, they play more quietly.

■ Oboes
■ Clarinets
■ Bassoons
□ Horns

□ Trumpets
□ Trombones
□ Tubas
■ Percussion

The Symphony

The word *symphony* simply means sounding together. For 200 years, from about 1750, the most important piece of music a composer could write was a symphony. Orchestras are called symphony orchestras because originally they were developed to cope with the kind of music composers were writing in their symphonies. What is a symphony, and how did it begin? The story of the symphony starts when operas – dramatic stories set to music – were first becoming popular. For opera composers in the 17th and 18th centuries, a symphony was any piece of instrumental music played between the sung parts of the opera, especially the music at the beginning, called an overture.

In Italy, overtures had three sections: a fast, catchy one to begin with, then a slower one, and often, a fast final one. Sometimes, this last one would be a minuet. The three sections of the overture soon split off from each other and became completely separate movements. Gradually, symphonies (or overtures as they were often still called) settled down to a regular four-movement pattern. There was a fast first movement, a slow second, a minuet for the third movement, and a fast finale.

Great symphony writers

Haydn was the first great composer of symphonies. Mozart followed his example, and Beethoven learned from them both. All three composers happened to be living in Vienna, Austria (a famous center for music) at about the same time. Ever since, the most important symphonists have worked there, including Franz Schubert, Johannes Brahms, Anton Bruckner, and Gustav Mahler.

It was Beethoven, though, who showed what symphonies could really do. He made his symphonies express the great excitement people were feeling at the time, when the French Revolution seemed to be promising freedom to so many people. He even dedicated his third symphony to Napoleon; but, when he heard Napoleon had crowned himself emperor, he tore up the page. It still sounds heroic, though, and is called the *Eroica* (or *Heroic*) *Symphony*. Most symphonies are not meant to describe any person or event. Those which do are usually called symphonic poems. Richard Strauss's *Alpine Symphony* and *Don Quixote*, mentioned on pages 26 and 27, are really two of these.

The shape of a symphony

A symphony is very like a play: it is a drama in music, a play of great musical ideas. Most of the drama goes on in the first movement, which is designed in a special way, called sonata form. The two basic shapes at the beginning are brought into close

Above: A detail from Jacques-Louis David's painting of the coronation of Napoleon. Napoleon is seen crowning his Empress Josephine. When Beethoven heard about the coronation, he angrily tore up the score of his third symphony.

contact in the middle and then everything is brought back into order by the end. The two patterns stand for two tunes, or themes, which are brought together in the middle of a symphony in a series of more complicated musical ideas – similar to two characters arguing with each other in a play.

Two of Beethoven's most famous symphonies, his third and fifth, show this pattern very

clearly. They all start with a bold first tune, called the first subject. Then, there is a contrasting group of tunes called the second subject. The middle section, where the tunes are brought together, is called a development, because the composer tries his themes out to see how he can make them change or develop, suggest other ideas, and add to the excitement. The last section, in which the first and second

subjects are repeated in the form they were in at the start, is called the recapitulation. Beethoven's fifth symphony is the clearest. The very famous first four notes really give the composer all he needs. He builds those notes up into a strong first subject and even uses the same rhythm on the horns to start the second one. As a complete contrast, the second movement is slow and song-like. In this symphony, though, Beethoven turns the minuet into a movement so fast you couldn't possibly dance to it! This is called a scherzo, which is designed to get the pulses racing again. The finale keeps up the pace, but Beethoven often uses the same design as the first movement to end a symphony at a high level of dramatic excitement.

Above: The first page of Beethoven's *Symphony No 5*. Notice how the score starts with some of the woodwinds, then the brass, timpani, and strings join in. Can you see the shape of the famous opening tune?

Above: Ludwig van Beethoven (1770–1827) carried notebooks around to "sketch" tunes to work on at a later date.

Building Patterns

On pages 30 and 31, you read about music which does not imitate or describe anything directly. When you listen to it, pictures might come into your head, but the composers were usually just thinking of the sounds when they wrote the music. This kind of music is called abstract music. There are also abstract paintings. Just as an abstract painter builds up patterns of shape and color on a canvas, so an abstract composer builds patterns of notes and instrumental color in his music.

When Johann Sebastian Bach was writing music, about 250 years ago, people admired elegant style and pattern. Buildings, particularly churches, were decorated with very complicated designs. Organs in the churches were built with careful attention to the balance of pipework. In the photograph (right), you can see how all the ranks of pipes are grouped into intricate patterns.

Patterns in music

Similar patterns were reflected in the music of the time. At the bottom of the page is part of the *Toccata and Fugue in D Minor* by Bach. The composer makes a striking start to the toccata: the first note with the sign above it is a high, loud "twiddle" which catches our attention, and makes us wait eagerly for what follows. The run of short, fast notes that comes next is a surprising contrast. Bach then repeats the pattern at a lower pitch, slightly altering it, as well. Then, Bach builds a new line made up of a new pattern. This kind of thing happens all the way through the toccata. *Toccata* is the Italian word for touched, and describes a piece in which players show how well they can use their skill of touch.

A fugue is another kind of musical pattern-making. It starts with a tune called the subject. Then, as in a round such as *Frère Jacques*, another voice or instrument (or on keyboard instruments, another hand) takes up the subject, and the first voice builds up patterns around it.

The concerto

Musical patterns can sound very exciting, when the composer juggles with high and low notes, long or short notes, or groups of notes. Instruments can play against each other, or a solo melody can be contrasted against another played with many instruments blending with one another. This is the basis of concerto form. A concerto in Bach's day played different groups of instruments against each other as well as showing them off as solo instruments. In the beginning of the score of Bach's second Brandenburg concerto, the notes, put together, form different shapes, and the tune is built up of groups of these shapes. The notes are like bricks making patterns in a wall. The trumpet's notes make up one wall of a house, which is added to by each of the other instruments, so that the whole piece of music can be thought of as a building.

Since about 1918, composers have been writing abstract music again. The Russian, Igor Stravinsky, and the German, Paul Hindemith, are the most important composers of this kind of music.

Serial music

A different type of pattern-making was invented by Arnold Schönberg. He organized the 12 semi-tones of the octave into a

Above: Johann Sebastian Bach (1685–1750)

Right: The beginning of Bach's *Toccata and Fugue in D minor*. Can you work out the boy's expressions as he listens to it?

series, which then formed the basis for a whole composition. This is called serial music, or sometimes 12-note music. Often, the music is built up of little cells of notes, such as his piano pieces written in 1909.

Right: The 18th-century organ in Göttweig Abbey, Austria. Each group of pipes is controlled by a stop, and each rank of pipes makes a different quality of sound in the same way as instruments in an orchestra.

Above: Arnold Schönberg (1874–1951)

Singing Together

You have read how important it was for people to sing. Many people like singing in groups; large groups such as choirs, or small ones such as barbershop quartets or the groups that used to gather around the piano in the past. In the princely households of the 15th, 16th, and 17th centuries, the most important form of group vocal music was the madrigal. This could be sung by any number of singers from two to ten, with or without the accompaniment of lutes or viols. The songs were usually love poems, but also often described hunts or battles. The music often took its cue from the words and imitated hunting horns, bird calls, or street cries. Sometimes, the music illustrated words such as *fall*, *flowing river*, or *mountains*, by making the notes drop down, flow smoothly, or rise up and down. The English madrigalists learned their art from the Italians. Englishmen such as William Byrd and Orlando Gibbons raised it to a high peak.

Splendid masques

Meanwhile, men such as Claudio Monteverdi in Italy were starting new kinds of songwriting. Another development of the madrigal in Italy was to string a series of them together to tell a story. This madrigal comedy was acted out, and eventually led to the first operas, which appeared about 1600. Musical stories were also told in the form of a masque in many courts in Europe. In a masque, the whole court danced, sang, and acted out a well-known story or myth from ancient history. Gradually, masques were brought in as interludes in theatrical presentations.

Henry Purcell was one of the greatest composers of such works. His own teacher, John Blow, gave up his position as organist of Westminster Abbey for him. Purcell's vocal music has for long been regarded as the greatest example of setting words to music in English, the art of finding the most suitable rhythm or melodies to match the meaning and

expression of a word. Purcell composed the first real English opera, called *Dido and Aeneas*, for a girls' school.

Songs of praise

By the time the great composer George Frideric Handel settled in London, Purcell was dead, but

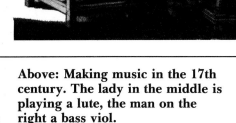

Above: Making music in the 17th century. The lady in the middle is playing a lute, the man on the right a bass viol.

Right: A courtly masque at an Elizabethan wedding. The musicians are playing a flute (left) and a viol (right).

Handel was still greatly influenced by Purcell's music. Handel wrote many pieces of music for the large choirs in English churches and courts. Although he came to England as an opera composer, he began to compose a whole series of oratorios to be performed during Lent, when the Church did not allow operas to be performed. An oratorio tells a story, usually on a religious subject, but it is not acted in the same way as an opera. The most famous oratorio is Handel's *Messiah*.

For the 250 years since Handel's day, oratorio has been a very important form in English music. Later, composers were inspired by Handel's example to compose some of their greatest works after visiting England, where nearly every town had a choral society as well as an orchestra. Haydn wrote *The Creation* and *The Seasons*, and Mendelssohn wrote *Elijah*. Edward Elgar gave the oratorio a new lease of life in Britain in the 1900s with works such as *The Dream of Gerontius* and *The Apostles*. Later, Benjamin Britten developed British choral music, but usually for smaller groups than the 200 singers needed in a 19th-century oratorio. Britten was greatly influenced by Purcell, and his *Young Persons' Guide to the Orchestra* is based on a theme from a Purcell dance. He wrote several pieces to be performed in church, some for children like *Noye's Fludde*. Others, called *Parables for Church Performance*, imitate Japanese plays. He also wrote many operas.

Above: George Frideric Handel (1685–1759) was German, but his work influenced English music for 100 years.

Singing a Story

The word *opera* covers many different styles of music. The one thing they all have in common is a story, acted out on stage by singers accompanied by a group of instrumentalists. Operas can be short and simple, or they can be very long and complicated. Large operas need huge orchestras, choruses, many singers and dancers, and large stages with a great deal of scenery and the technicians to operate it. Some operas are sung all the way through; in others, characters speak between the songs.

Opera began in Italy around 1600. Monteverdi was the first great opera composer. By the 1700s, there were two basic styles in Italy; *seria* or serious opera, and *buffa* or comic opera. Handel wrote in the seria style, but by the end of the century, Mozart had brought the two styles together. His operas, such as *The Marriage of Figaro* and *Don Giovanni*, have both serious and comic elements. Another style that was developed in France and Germany was the *Singspiel*, or sungplay, in which spoken dialogue is used between songs. *The Magic Flute*, Mozart's last opera, and Beethoven's only one, *Fidelio*, are in this style.

Musical mascots

In the 19th century, the opera world split into two camps, the Italian one led by Giuseppe Verdi and the German one led by Richard Wagner. The Italians developed the art of singing, and wrote music that was designed to show off the voice. The Germans wrote symphonic operas, where the music was composed with the same principles of development as a symphony. The split in the opera world was wide because Italian nationalists adopted Verdi as a mascot, while Wagner was heavily involved in politics and revolution in Germany.

The Italians scrawled Verdi's name on walls as a code because it stood for *Victor Emanuel Re d'Italia*, the king who they hoped would unite Italy and throw out foreign rulers. Verdi was born in 1813, the same year as Wagner. One of his most famous operas is *Aida*, which tells the story of an Ethiopian princess who falls in love with an Egyptian general.

Out of love for her, he betrays the Egyptian army and is buried alive with her under a pyramid. *Aida* was written to celebrate the opening of the Suez Canal and was first performed in Cairo. There is a famous triumphal march in *Aida* which needs many singers and dancers.

The story of The Ring

Wagner also wrote at a time when all the German states were beginning to feel the need to unite. Four of his operas are intended to be performed as a series. They tell the old mythological story of the *Ring of*

Above: Giuseppe Verdi (1813–1901)

Above: Richard Wagner (1813–1883)

Left: As the three Norns weave the thread of fate in _The Twilight of the Gods_, it breaks and they know the end of the old world is near.

the Nibelung. The Ring is made from gold, stolen from the bottom of the Rhine River by the dwarf Alberich. He hopes to rule the world with its power, but Wotan, king of the gods, creates a race of heroes to conquer him and bring a new era of justice. This was Wagner's way of criticizing the evils around him.

There is plenty of action in the fourth and last opera, _The Twilight of the Gods_. The hero, Siegfried, is drugged by Alberich's son, Hagen, into betraying his love, Brunnhilde, and wants to marry another woman. When Siegfried realizes what has happened, Hagen kills him and tries to steal the Ring for himself. Brunnhilde stops him and throws herself onto Siegfried's funeral pyre. The waters of the Rhine swell up and, destroying the old world, win back the Ring.

Not many operas need as many people to perform them as _Aida_ or _The Ring_. Mozart's operas, such as _The Magic Flute_ which is described on page 25, use smaller orchestras. Most of Handel's operas have no chorus. Modern composers, such as Benjamin Britten (see page 35), have written for smaller numbers of performers than Verdi or Wagner. These operas can be performed quite cheaply, in small theaters. They can be produced anywhere where there is enough space for performers and audience.

Left: Radames, the Egyptian general, arrives at the Pharoah's court after his victory over the Ethiopians in _Aida_.

Dancing a Story

Elegant dances were developed at the French court in the middle of the 17th century. Also, early French opera always had an important element of ballet – that is why most ballet terms are French words. By the middle of the 19th century, though, Russia had become the center of dance, and this continued right into the middle of the 20th century. Two composers, Peter Tchaikovsky and Igor Stravinsky, are particularly associated with the history of ballet over the last hundred years.

The start of modern ballet
The three ballet scores of Tchaikovsky, *Sleeping Beauty*, *Swan Lake*, and *The Nutcracker*, are undoubtedly the most popular ever written. His rich melody and brilliant use of the orchestra seem to match the magic of the ballets. Russian music in general had not made a great impact before Tchaikovsky, but after him a whole new group of brilliant composers emerged.

Left: Peter Ilyich Tchaikovsky (1840–1893)

Above: A scene from a performance of Tchaikovsky's last ballet, *The Nutcracker*. This ballet tells the story of a nutcracker given as a present to a girl, Clara. Clara dreams that the nutcracker turns into a prince who takes her on a fabulous journey. These dancers are "snowflakes" that they meet in the Land of Snow on the way to their journey's end.

Tchaikovsky wrote many operas, some (such as *Eugene Onegin*) with famous dance scenes. He also wrote powerful symphonies as well as works for solo piano, voice, and violin.

Just as in opera, the main action of a ballet story is danced by solo dancers in the character parts. There is also a *corps de ballet*, the dance equivalent of the chorus in an opera, who usually take the part of crowds, courtiers, armies, and servants. Just as most large cities have their own choral society and orchestra, they often have a ballet company.

Brilliant partners

Early in the 20th century, the Russian impresario Sergei Diaghilev traveled throughout Europe with a Russian ballet company. He invited Igor Stravinsky to write some music for a new ballet, *The Firebird*. Stravinsky's first three ballets, *The Firebird*, *Petrushka*, and *The Rite of Spring*, are not danced very often because of their extreme difficulty, but their music is among his most popular. There was a riot at the first performance of *The Rite of Spring*. The audience was outraged by what it considered Stravinsky's discordant harmonies and jagged rhythms, which describe a pagan ceremony when a young girl dances herself to death to make the land give a good harvest.

The Firebird

The Firebird was more acceptable, and it remains one of Stravinsky's richest scores. It tells the story of the Firebird, who gives the Prince one of her feathers to call her when he is in danger. The Prince uses the feather to call the Firebird to help him rescue the Tsar's daughter, whom he then marries. Stravinsky wrote many other ballets. One of them, *The Fairy's Kiss*, is based on melodies by Tchaikovsky. Like Tchaikovsky, Stravinsky also wrote symphonies, operas, and works for piano and violin in addition to his 12 ballets. During that time, he was regarded as the most important composer of the century.

Above: A scene from *The Firebird* by Stravinsky. Prince Ivan has captured the Firebird and only lets her go when she gives him one of her feathers. The music she dances to, and the choreography, or dance design, make her seem like a real bird.

Above: Igor Stravinsky (1882–1971). His ballet music is so interesting it is often played in concerts without dancers.

Musical Backdrops

In addition to opera and ballet, music plays another important part in the theater. Many other plays need music at some time or another. It helps put an audience in the right mood by suggesting the atmosphere of a scene of action, such as night or a storm. It can break the mood of one scene to move into another, and cover up long and difficult scene changes so that an audience remains in the right frame of mind. Quite often, there are songs, too, which need instrumental accompaniment. This kind of music is called incidental music.

Music for plays

Today, most incidental music is recorded and played on records or tapes, but sometimes larger theaters hire small groups of musicians for their plays, especially if there is much singing. In earlier times, though, most theaters had their own orchestras. The incidental music Felix Mendelssohn wrote for a production of Shakespeare's *A Midsummer Night's Dream* is where the famous *Wedding March* comes from. At the top of the next page, you can see the fairy queen and attendants in a scene from the play. Beethoven's music for *Egmont* by Goethe needed a full symphony orchestra and a chorus, and is regarded as a very important part of the composer's work.

When composers wrote for plays, they usually composed a full-scale overture just as for an opera. Then, they wrote various pieces, called *intermezzos*, to go between the scenes and *entr'actes*, between the acts. If music was needed to accompany speech, it was called a melodrama. Some of the most popular music by many composers has been written as incidental music for plays, and is often the only reason some plays are remembered. Music such as that which Franz Schubert wrote for *Rosamunde*, Frederick Delius for *Hassan*, and Ralph Vaughan Williams for *The Wasps* are examples.

The story of Peer Gynt

Perhaps the most famous incidental music ever written was that which Edvard Grieg wrote for Ibsen's play *Peer Gynt*, and includes *In the Hall of the Mountain King*. Ibsen's play is already a very long one, but it would last nearly nine hours with all Grieg's music. It tells of the wanderings of Peer Gynt throughout the world in search of love and adventure, before returning home to die in the arms of Solveig, the woman who had always loved him.

Music for Finland

Another European composer of incidental music is the Finnish composer, Jean Sibelius. Right from the start, Sibelius set out to write music to make his countrymen proud to be Finnish. His *Karelia* music was among his earliest and remains his most popular. (Karelia is a province of South Finland.) He also wrote symphonic poems describing stories from Finnish folklore, such as the *Swan of Tuonela*, or the *Lemminkäinen Legends*, and incidental music for a production of Shakespeare's *The Tempest*.

Above: Edvard Grieg (1843–1907) was a fine pianist, and his piano concerto is one of the most popular there is.

Above: A still from the 1981 movie, *Chariots of Fire*. The movie soundtrack, by Vangelis, won an Academy Award.

Above: Jean Sibelius
(1865–1957)
Above left: Titania, the fairy
in *A Midsummer Night's Dream.*

Film music

Another branch of incidental music is film music. In the early days of moviemaking, silent movies were accompanied by live piano music. "Talkies," or sound movies, appeared in 1927, but it was not until the late 1930s that film directors began to think seriously about the connection between cinematic rhythm and musical rhythm. Since then, many famous composers have written original musical scores for movies, including Aaron Copland, Sergei Prokofiev, and Benjamin Britten. Film music can also be an adaption of an existing musical work, such as Stanley Kubrick's use of György Ligeti's *Requiem* and Richard Strauss's *Also sprach Zarathustra* in the movie *2001: A Space Odyssey.* Today, movie soundtrack albums are among the biggest-selling records every year.

Musical Suggestions

Sibelius's prelude to *The Tempest* suggests a storm at sea. The movement of the notes, the busy rise and fall, the thickness of the sound, the dark and shrill color of the instruments Sibelius uses, all give the unmistakable impression of a storm.

Imitating real sounds

Music can imitate things such as church bells, cowbells or bird calls almost exactly. Composers can also use recordings of everyday sounds to color their music. For the hundreds of years before tape recorders were invented, though, musicians enjoyed trying to imitate such things as sea battles, storms, and hunts. The German composer Johann Kuhnau told the story of David and Goliath in one of his *Biblical Sonatas*. People enjoyed listening to the clever way the composer used various instruments to imitate the sounds of the battle that takes place between the hero David and the giant, Goliath.

Program music, as it is called, was always an important part of French music. In their keyboard music, Couperin and Rameau invented a great deal of fanciful titles for each movement, such as *Les Tricoteuses* (*The Knitting Women*) or *Les Barricades Mystérieuses* (*The Mysterious Barricades*). By the time Debussy and Ravel were writing music 200 years later, Berlioz, Liszt, and Strauss had all made brave attempts to write program music, describing everything from a witches' Sabbath to St. Francis walking on the waters or Don Quixote fighting sheep.

The color of sound

Debussy, though, had a fine appreciation of sound for its own sake, just as Impressionist painters were more interested in light than the objects it helped them to see. Much impressionist music simply describes pictures or scenes, but most of Debussy's music uses the title of a piece as a starting point for interesting musical explorations of sounds for their own sakes. The development of the piano had a lot to do with it. It had become an adaptable, expressive instrument that could conjure up worlds of magical sound. It was almost as if different chords, or combinations of notes, had a color and meaning of their own. See if you can create different-colored sounds by experimenting on a keyboard. Watery effects are easy to get, but you can also make brilliant, bright chords or short, sharp, jagged ones, or warm or somber ones that are dark in color. What colors do your sounds suggest? Write

Above right: Claude Debussy (1862–1918) worked hard to create a certain impression or feeling in his music.

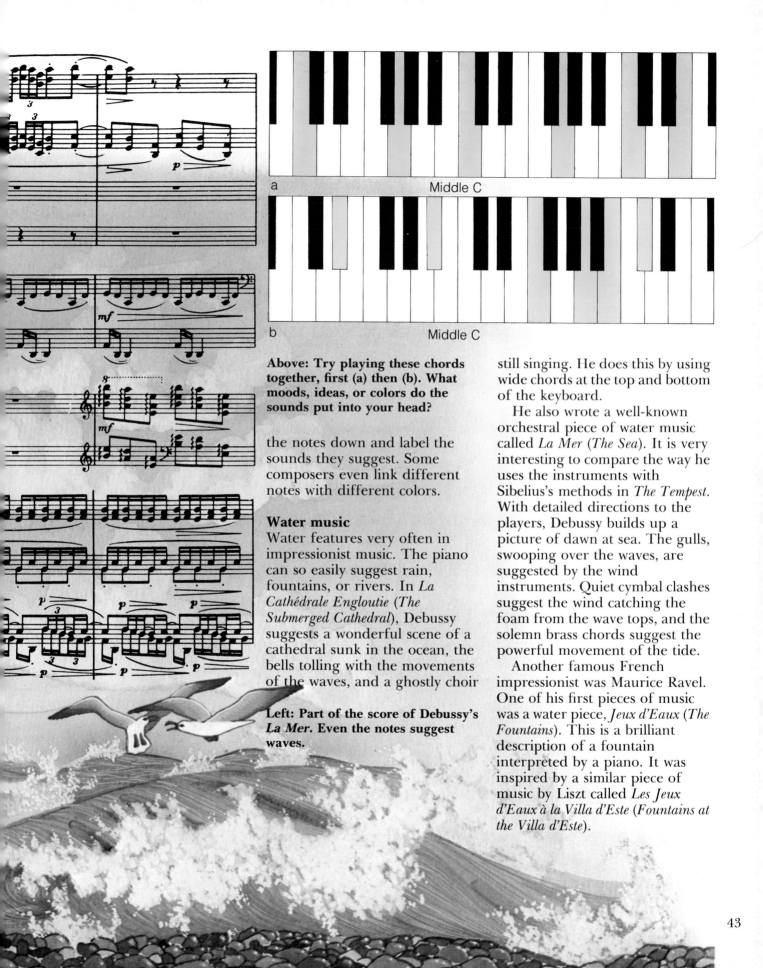

Above: Try playing these chords together, first (a) then (b). What moods, ideas, or colors do the sounds put into your head?

the notes down and label the sounds they suggest. Some composers even link different notes with different colors.

Water music

Water features very often in impressionist music. The piano can so easily suggest rain, fountains, or rivers. In *La Cathédrale Engloutie* (*The Submerged Cathedral*), Debussy suggests a wonderful scene of a cathedral sunk in the ocean, the bells tolling with the movements of the waves, and a ghostly choir

Left: Part of the score of Debussy's *La Mer*. Even the notes suggest waves.

still singing. He does this by using wide chords at the top and bottom of the keyboard.

He also wrote a well-known orchestral piece of water music called *La Mer* (*The Sea*). It is very interesting to compare the way he uses the instruments with Sibelius's methods in *The Tempest*. With detailed directions to the players, Debussy builds up a picture of dawn at sea. The gulls, swooping over the waves, are suggested by the wind instruments. Quiet cymbal clashes suggest the wind catching the foam from the wave tops, and the solemn brass chords suggest the powerful movement of the tide.

Another famous French impressionist was Maurice Ravel. One of his first pieces of music was a water piece, *Jeux d'Eaux* (*The Fountains*). This is a brilliant description of a fountain interpreted by a piano. It was inspired by a similar piece of music by Liszt called *Les Jeux d'Eaux à la Villa d'Este* (*Fountains at the Villa d'Este*).

Masters of Music

As you read at the beginning of the book, anybody can write some kind of music and many do. Only a few composers, though, have done it so well and so differently that they catch people's imaginations and make them wonder what the world could have been like without such music. Each composer, in his or her own way, has developed the way we listen, the way we think and feel, and how we act in our daily lives. Each important composer has made a major contribution to at least one form of music: opera, ballet, chamber or piano music, song, the symphony, choral music – all the various types of music that you have read about. Hundreds of composers have inspired millions of people over the centuries; these, together with others whom you have read about in the book, are a few of the composers who have played an important part in the story of music.

The composers pictured here and in the rest of *Listening to Music* span more than 400 years of musical history. Music has changed a great deal in that period. In the 16th century, most people had a clear idea of what they thought music was – it would not have included anything Karlheinz Stockhausen calls music today, but, of course, electronics had not been invented. New instruments mean new sounds, new methods of composing, and new music. Each of these men, in his own way, wrote the best music of its type. They all kept their ears and minds open, and thought about what they heard. You can, too!

**William Byrd
(c. 1542–1623)**

**Henry Purcell
(1659–1695)**

**Johannes Brahms
(1833–1897)**

**Franz Liszt
(1811–1886)**

**Benjamin Britten
(1913–1976)**

Jean Philippe Rameau
(1683–1764)

Wolfgang Amadeus Mozart
(1756–1791)

Franz Schubert
(1797–1828)

Richard Strauss
(1864–1949)

Maurice Ravel
(1875–1937)

George Gershwin
(1898–1937)

Leonard Bernstein
(b. 1918)

What To Do Next

This book can only show you the tip of the musical iceberg. There is much more to discover about music, and many ways of doing it. You might want to play an instrument, join a choir, even compose your own music. You might just want to listen! Most of the world's successful musicians have started by getting their friends together to make music and perform it. You can do the same, turning everything around you into your own music.

Learning to play

If you want to learn an instrument, you can usually do it at school. Your music teacher can often arrange for you to borrow an instrument. Most schools have marching bands, concert bands, jazz bands, and special ensembles. Throughout the school year, bands perform regularly, and band members often compete in statewide band contests, either as a group or solo. Many communities also have bands or orchestras. Being in a band is hard work, but you can learn both your own instrument and how instruments sound together in a group.

The voice is an instrument, too. You might want to join the school choir or glee club, church choir, community chorus, or a special vocal ensemble. If you play an instrument, you might like to accompany a choir or solo singer. Your music teacher or band director at school is the best person to ask about the opportunities your school and community offer.

Learning to listen

You may want to explore the world of music simply by listening. But you can learn to be a better listener. You might want to go to a concert. As a student, you may be able to get inexpensive tickets. Before you go, visit the local library, and read about the music that you will be hearing and the composer who wrote it. You can even get miniature scores of the music, and follow it through as you listen to the performance.

Of course, the best way to get to know a piece of music is to buy it (or borrow it from the library) on record or tape, and have the score, too. Your library might have several versions of the same musical work. See if you can listen to them and compare how each conductor and orchestra interprets the music. Read the liner notes on the record covers, too; they can help you to learn more about the music.

You may want to join a music appreciation club. Sometimes, professional musicians come and talk to club members. Clubs exist, too, for opera and ballet lovers, and they can often organize visits to the backstage area of a theater and to dress rehearsals of operas and ballets.

You might hope to turn your love for music into a career. To become a professional musician, you generally need to have had some experience of music making, either playing, singing, or composing; to have learned an instrument; and then to have gone to one of the many music conservatories or degree programs at a university. Your music teacher can usually give you advice on what would be your best course of action.

The answer to the puzzle on pages 14–15 is:
Cabbage-faced deaf dad bagged a faded aged cab.

Glossary

chamber music Instrumental music written for performance in a small room, usually having one player for each part.

development In **sonata form**, the elaboration of the musical theme set forth in the **exposition**.

dynamics The degree and contrast of loudness and softness.

entr'actes (French) A piece of music played between acts of a play, or during the intermission.

exposition The first part of a musical work in **sonata form**, in which the theme is presented.

fugue A piece of music in which one or two themes are repeated and developed by voices or parts entering in succession.

fundamental note The principal musical tone produced by vibration on which a series of higher **harmonics** is based.

harmonics Tones produced by the frequencies of vibrations which are a multiple of that of the **fundamental note**.

incidental music Descriptive music played during a play, movie, etc., to project a mood or to accompany action.

intermezzo (Italian) Short musical piece played between the major sections of an **opera**.

metronome Instrument to mark exact time by a regularly repeated "tick."

movement A distinct division of a longer piece of music, with its own key, **rhythm**, and theme.

neumes Symbols used in the notation of medieval church music.

opera A drama set to music. The story is sung rather than spoken, with orchestral accompaniment.

oratorio Choral work, usually written about a religious topic.

overture The orchestral introduction to a musical dramatic work. Or, a one-movement orchestral work.

percussion Family of musical instruments sounded by striking, shaking, or scraping.

program music Music written to suggest a sequence of images, ideas, or events.

recapitulation The third section in **sonata form**, in which the original theme is repeated.

resonance The ability to continue to sound.

rhythm The accentuation and distribution of notes and spaces in music.

scherzo Lively musical movement or composition, usually in quick triple time.

sonata form Musical form made up of an **exposition**, a **development**, and a **recapitulation**.

string quartet Four performers playing string instruments, usually first and second violins, a viola, and a cello.

symphonic poem Orchestral work based on a non-musical inspiration; usually freer in form than a **symphony**.

symphony Long and complex sonata for a symphony orchestra. Most symphonies have four **movements**. Or, sometimes used as a shortened name for a symphony orchestra.

tangent Small metal pin that strikes the string on a clavichord to produce noise.

tocatta Musical form characterized by full chords and high harmonies.

Bibliography

Buxton, David and Sue Lyon, eds. *The Great Composers: Their Lives and Times.* 10 vols. Marshall Cavendish Corporation (Freeport, 1987).

Diagram Group. *The Scribner Guide to Orchestral Instruments.* Scribner (New York, 1983).

Machlis, Joseph. *The Enjoyment of Music: An Introduction to Perceptive Listening.* W. W. Norton (New York, 1984).

McLeish, Kenneth and Valerie. *Music Round The World.* Oxford University Press (New York, 1982).

McLeish, Kenneth and Valerie. *The Oxford First Companion to Music.* Oxford University Press (New York, 1982).

Previn, André, ed. *André Previn's Guide to the Orchestra.* Putnam (New York, 1983).

Index

Picture Credits

Illustrations
pp 4–5 Jane Walton; p 6 Tom Stimpson; pp 10–11 Juliet Stanwell-Smith; p 13 Barbara Howes; p 16 Jane Walton; p 17 Jane Walton; p 19 Juliet Stanwell-Smith; p 20 Tom Stimpson; p 22 Juliet Stanwell-Smith; p 24(BR) Juliet Stanwell-Smith; p 24(BL,T) Tom Stimpson; pp 26–27 Tom Stimpson; pp 28–29 Tony Streak; pp 32–33 Malcolm Livingstone; pp 42–43 Jane Walton; p 46 Juliet Stanwell-Smith.

Photographs
p 6 Courtesy of the Trustees of the British Museum; p 7 Stephen Benson; pp 8–9(T) Courtesy of the Turkish Ministry of Tourism and Information; pp 8–9(B) British Tourist Authority; p 9(L) Jack Blake; p 9(R) Mansell Collection; pp 10–11 Universal Edition, London, Ltd.; p 12(T) Royal College of Music; p 12(B) Eileen Tweedy/Science Museum; pp 12–13 Kobal Collection/United Artists Film Corporation; p 14 Bodleian Library; p 15 Mary Evans Picture Library; pp 16–17 Universal Edition, London, Ltd.; pp 18–19 Alan Duns; pp 20–21 Courtesy of John Broadwood and Sons Ltd.; p 21(T) Mansell Collection; p 21(B) Victoria and Albert Museum; p 22 Sophie Baker; pp 22–23 Alan Duns; pp 24–25 Alan Duns; p 25 Reg Wilson; pp 26–27 Alan Duns; pp 28–29 Drawings from *The Maestro* by Gerald Hoffnung, Dobson Books Ltd.; p 30 Scala; p 31(L) Courtesy of Peters Edition, London, New York, Frankfurt; p 31(R) John Lee; p 32 John Lee; pp 32–33 Courtesy of Peters Edition, London, New York, Frankfurt; p 33(L) Universal Edition, London, Ltd.; p 33(R) A.F. Kersting; p 34 John Lee; pp 34–35 National Portrait Gallery; p 35 Mansell Collection; p 36(L) Mansell Collection; p 36(R) Victoria and Albert Museum/Theatre Museum; pp 36–37 Reg Wilson; p 37 Reg Wilson; p 38(T) Radio Times Hulton Picture Library; p 38(B) Reg Wilson; p 39(L) Reg Wilson; p 39(R) Erich Auerbach; p 40 Mansell Collection; pp 40–41 By permission of 20th Century Fox; p 41(L) Joe Cocks; p 41(R) Mary Evans Picture Library; p 42 Mansell Collection; p 44(TL) Mansell Collection; p 44(TR) Victoria and Albert Museum/Theatre Museum; p 44(CL) Mary Evans Picture Library; p 44(BR) Royal College of Music; p 44(BL) Courtesy of the Decca Record Company Ltd.; p 45(TL) Mansell Collection; p 45(TC) John Lee; p 45(TR) Mansell Collection; p 45 (CL) Radio Times Hulton Picture Library; p 45(C) Radio Times Hulton Picture Library; p 45(BL) Deutsche Gramophone Production; Front cover *Boy Playing Flute* by Judith Leyster, National Museum, Stockholm.